Coloring Outside The Lines

Shaniqua Davis

BookLeaf Publishing

Presentation by *BookLeaf Publishing*

Web: www.bookleafpub.com

E-mail: info@bookleafpub.com

ISBN: 9789358736670

First edition 2023

Dedicated to a few people ...

"To my Minions, you guys are the sunshine that brightens my days and the stars that illuminate my nights"

"To my Pop, who always pushes me to reach for the stars"

"To myself, for showing up, pushing through, and finishing what I started"

"To all those who pick up this book, thank you for giving my words a chance"

ACKNOWLEDGEMENT

First, I want to thank the Higher Power for waking me up everyday to live this life so that I can write about it, from the good and bad times to the happy and sad moments. Next, family is where all journeys start and I've been blessed with the best little tribe. I want to thank my tribe for always supporting, loving, and understanding because it has helped me become who I am today. Lastly, I want to send a bunch of thanks to the publishing company (Bookleaf Publishing) for giving me an opportunity to be a part of their challenge. This whole experience has been fun and exciting, the part where I got back into writing to the part where I would hold a book with my name as the author.

PREFACE

I was scrolling on social media and saw a 21 Day Poem Challenge called #TheWriteAngle, I was super intrigued even though I hadn't written a poem in over 10 years. I felt nervous at the thought of writing, but I'm no punk, so I accepted the challenge and my brain started to flood with all these new things that I could write about and add them to what I already had in my archives. Once I started writing, it felt good to play with words again and the more poems I wrote, it was nice to see and hear my evolution as a writer. I am most glad I came across that social media posting, because it led me back to writing and in the end, I can be proud a book with my words was printed.

My Lucky Charm

My Lucky Charm
Is soft and cuddly,
It can come in different shapes, sizes, colors,
Also,
It can come with different sayings like:
"I Love You" "Thank You" "Best Friends"
Can you guess what My Lucky charm is?
My Lucky Charm is …
A Teddy Bear !!

The Man I Never Knew

Where are you?
Why have you gone away?
How come you did not want to stay?

Dad, you need to know
I am growing up
Dad, you need to understand
You are the only person I will never ever know
Dad, you need to think
About what you did and why you did it

Even though you cannot,
I wish you could feel the pain
I felt once I realized you were not there
Half of my heart disappeared,
The moment you left

Dad, I need to know
Where are you?
Why have you gone away?
How come you did not want to stay?

Thank You

You can say thank you to anyone
You can say thank you for anything
But there is one person that I want to respond to
…
There is one line this person has said and done
"I'm going to take you in and care for you as
long as I live"
That line is still being done today
…
That person that I would like to respond to is
My Grandmother AKA Nana
Thank You!!

The Lady Before Me

I have a question …
"What happened to you??"
You need to answer so you can know your damn
self
Everybody knows except you, and you need to
catch up

You need to sit and think …
Who? To me, this is about you
What happened? Don't ask me, but some say it
was a big deal
When did it happen? To me, it happens everyday
Where did it happen? Don't ask me, but some
say everywhere
Why did it happen? To me, you don't change
anything, so you get the same result

Once you can answer all those questions,
Go and think about what I asked earlier,
And you will know …
"What happened to you??"

Bonded

There is a four-letter word that means
Happiness
This word is Love
Being in love, is the most beautiful thing in the
world
The best part is knowing that your person loves
you back
That love can last forever
Until
There is a four-letter word that means
Sadness
This word is Pain
Being in pain, is the most miserable thing in the
world
The worst part is knowing your person was with
someone else
That pain will last forever

Broken

A broken heart
hurts like hell
A broken heart
means the love as fell
A broken heart
is too painful to bare
A broken heart
just isn't fair
A broken heart
is something nobody wants
But unfortunately
it is what I have

A Little Girl

Everybody loves her for who she is
This little girl is a sweetheart,
She is quiet,
She doesn't bother anyone,
She isn't violent at all,
But that's about to change …

People started to annoy her and she snapped
That little girl became very angry on the inside,
She became very mean,
She didn't like people at all,
She started punching walls,
The sweetheart was locked away, almost gone

One day she learned how to control her
emotions
That angry little girl appears when she is needed
Now she is happy with herself and the life she
lives
This little girl is …
Me

Wish

A boy meets a girl
They become friends
Argue and fight but remain the same
Suddenly, the boy reveals a feeling
Then the girl does the same
They become lovers and friends
Argue and fight but remain the same
Suddenly, the boy says three words
Then the girl does the same
There is something wrong
She wants him to herself
But …
They are a secret
Her wish will never come true

Feels

I get this feeling
Every time I see him
I get this feeling
Every time I hear him
I get this feeling
Every time I touch him
I get this feeling
Every time I taste him
I get this feeling
Every time I smell him
I get this feeling
Every time we are together
Sometimes I cannot describe this feeling
But I do know it feels good
This feeling is …
Euphoric
I do not ever want it or him to fade away

Nobody

There is a boy
His name is Nobody
No one knows why that is his name
He is quiet and shy,
He is not mean or rude,
He has manners,
He has friends,
He has everything any teen would want
But …
We are soon to find out why
His parents died two days ago
Before they died there was a big argument
Last thing his parents said was "You are going to
grow up to be a nobody"
He replied "Fine I don't need you"
Then came a crash
He felt so guilty, he kept the last word his
parents said …
Nobody

Our Journey

Life's an adventure, twisty and free
A tarp of moments, for you and me
In the morn of birth, we take our first breath
And step by step, we dance toward death
Each day's a chapter, a story untold
With tales of triumph and challenges daring
In laughter and tears, we find our way
Walking the path, regardless of the outcome
Through the seasons of joy and storms of gloom
Life teaches us lessons, beyond compare
We learn to love, hope, and dream
As we navigate this special space
Life's a gift, precious and limited
A chance to be kind, to love, to care
So, let us cling to each moment, hold it close
And cherish this beautiful momentary journey

Challenges, Forevermore

In the passage of time, we find our way
From the innocence of youth to the light of morn
Adulthood entices with its door open
A path of challenges, forevermore

Gone are the days of carefree fun
Replaced by responsibilities day and night
Yet with each challenge and every scar
We become the architects of who we are

Through trial and error, we learn to grow
Navigating life's currents with a steady hand
Adulthood's canvas, a masterpiece
As we chase our dreams through sun and moon

Though the path is uncertain, we walk it strong
For in the adult world, we truly belong
With hearts resilient and spirits blazing
We welcome the complexities of these adult
days

The Wicked & The Heroes

In shadows deep, where darkness lives
A tale of horror, darkness grows
Destroyers heart frozen
Their twisted minds, a story made public

They roam the night with deadly grace,
Leaving behind a haunting footprint
Innocence they sadistically take
A dreadful path that some may walk

But let us not dwell on their awful
Instead, remember those they've bled
The heroes who seek justice true
To stop the madness they look for

In the darkest depth, light must shine
To end this dominion of hurt
For in the face of evil's will
Goodness wins, always still

Dear Friend

To my close friend, so real and true
I dedicate these honest words to you
Through thick and thin, you've been by my side
In you I've found a friendship that's genuine

In moments of sadness, you lend a caring ear
Wiping away tears and melting away unease
In times of celebration, you dance with
happiness
Our friendship's a treasure, a rare gem

Your support and kindness, a comforting hug
During trying times, you're my safe space
In your company, I am blessed with unending
beauty
A loyal friend who can never be replaced

So, here's to the moments past, present, and
future
In this beautiful friendship, there's no room for
debate
Forever and always, till the very end
You're my best friend, my confidant, my dearest
friend

September

On the first day of school, excitement's in the air
New backpacks, new shoes, and neatly combed
hair
Children with butterflies, hearts flutter with glee
Embarking on a new experience filled with
possibility
Within the halls of learning, young minds take
flight
School is a beacon, an instructive light
With books and lessons, friendships that form
In the journey of knowledge, we learn from the
past
The first day of school is a moment in time
A chapter unfolding in life's grand design
With hope in their hearts and dreams running
free
Children embrace learning, as it is meant to be
Though tests may challenge and studies strain,
School is an adventure where we build our
brain
For in its embrace, we find knowledge sweet
thrill,
A path to our dreams on which we fulfill

Hope

In the depths of solitude, it begins to creep
A silent shadow, a secret you keep
Depression, a relentless, heavy rain
Falling silently, causing endless pain
It wraps you in a blanket of despair
Leaving you gasping in the suffocating air
Invisible chains, it looks to bind
Till you are lost in the jungle of your own mind
Remember you are never truly alone
In this battle, you can find a home
Through the darkest night, a glimmer will gleam
A ray of hope in the deepest of the dream
Seek the hand that is offered, do not let it go
For love and support, they will help you grow
Unity and courage, we find the way
To chase the shadows and bring back the day

Mommy Life

Parenthood, a quest so grand
A bond so strong, forever planned
From the first cry of a precious birth
To the laughter that fills our home's warm abode

In the eyes of our children, we see the world
In their dreams and hopes, our love is spread
Through sleepless nights and their growing
pains
We are forever connected, like coursing veins

A journey of patience, an art of grace
In parenthood's clutch, we find our place
In their happy and sad times, we stand alongside
Guiding them through life's ever-changing ride

Each day, a blank page, where memories are
drawn
In this journey of love, we awaken at dawn
Parenthood, a role both daunting and sweet
In their laughter and tears, our hearts find their
beat

Minions

Children, like fireflies in the summer night
Bring magic and wonder, so bright
Their laughter, an anthem in the air
In their joyful spirit, nothing compares

Their eyes, like stars, twinkle with ecstasy
As they explore each day and every day
In their small minds, the future a mystery
In their little hearts, a story of courage and
curiosity

With small hands, they touch the soul's deepest
part
In their laughter and tears, they hold a key to
heart
Children, in their innocence, remind us of what's
true
In their presence, we rediscover life anew

Let's cherish the children, so precious and dear
Their smiles, their hopes, their laughter so clear
In their world, where love and joy dance
My minions are the treasure of my life, my
walking heartbeats

Pop

To my dearest other half, love so true
In the oasis of life, my rose is you
With every passing year, our love has grown
In your arms, my heart has found its home

Through ups and downs, in joy and conflict,
You have been my partner, my love, my life
Your being brightens my darkest days
In your cuddle, all worries fade away

Your glee, a song that fills my spirit
With you, love's journey is my true ambition
In your presence, I am complete, I am full
You are the missing piece that makes me whole

You are my confidant, my partner, my friend
With you, love's adventure has no end
Through thick and thin, we will face it all
With you, my Pop, I stand tall

Revelation

In the depths of my soul, I set out to explore
A journey of self-discovery to learn and soar
Through my maze of thoughts, emotions, and
dreams
I sought to understand what my essence truly
means

I searched my heart in moments of doubt
Seeking answers within, to find the way out
In the mirror reflection, I gazed deep
To uncover the secrets my soul did keep

Through trials and tests, I learned to be strong
In the face of adversity, I found where I belong
With every step forward, a new truth revealed
Self-exploration, the journey that transforms the
world

In moments of silence, I heard my own voice
Whispering truths, giving me a choice
To accept my flaws, my quirks, and my fears
To find strength in vulnerability, and dry my
eyes

In this adventure of personal exploration, I
found the key
To unlock the potential that sets my soul free
To be authentically me, unapologetically so
In the grand story of life, I will continue to grow

www.ingramcontent.com/pod-product-compliance
Lightning Source LLC
Chambersburg PA
CBHW071246140726
47996CB00007B/2774